# Why was the Earth without Form, Void, and Dark?

by Marianne Manley

**Why was the Earth without Form, Void, and Dark?**
**© Copyright 2019 by Marianne Manley**

**Permission is granted to use any and all contents of this book.**
**All scripture references are taken from the King James Bible.**

**Special Kindle instruction:**
**Remember that the Kindle Fire can read the book aloud to you. Put the settings on text-to-read. Ear phones or a speaker can be plugged into the Kindle. The pictures can be enlarged with a reverse pinch.**

**I have always wanted to understand how God created the universe from God's word. I finally understand it much better after reading CREATION "IN THE BEGINNING" by Gary Paul Miller.**
**Mr. Miller does a masterful job clearly communicating what God said about how He created heaven and earth. He presents this truth in a systematic step-by-step way that is easy to follow. Truth really is stranger than fiction. I highly recommend this book. The picture of eternity, heaven, and earth on page 8 is from his (page 45) and is used by permission. I also had to use a picture from his cover on page 11, since I was not able to find one like it. His book is the best book I have ever read on the subject of why the earth was formless, void, and dark in Genesis 1:2. It has given me such peace and rest in my mind to understand these things. I have permission from the Millers to share this information.**

**CREATION "IN THE BEGINNING"**
**by Gary Paul Miller can be ordered from:**
**Grace Harbor Church**
**2822 Briarwood Drive. East**
**Arlington Heights, IL 60005**
**847-640-8422**
**www.grace-harbor-church.org**

## CONTENTS

Introduction ............................................................................. 4
Eternity .................................................................................... 6
1. Heaven ................................................................................ 7
2. Angels ................................................................................. 8
3. Earth ................................................................................... 9
God's Plan for Heaven and Earth ........................................ 13
How did Rebellion Begin in Heaven? .................................. 14
The 7 Days ............................................................................ 16
How did Rebellion Begin on Earth? ..................................... 20
Adam and Eve Disobey God ................................................ 24
Adam and Eve Tried to Hide from God ............................... 25
Adam and Eve Have to Leave the Garden of Eden ............ 27
Adam and Eve had Cain and Abel ....................................... 29
Adam and Eve had More Children ...................................... 30
Exactly When did Adam and Eve Sin? ................................ 30
What is the Last Piece to this Puzzle? ................................. 32
Other Books by Marianne Manley ....................................... 37

# Introduction

In this short book we will not only attempt to understand how God created the heaven and the earth, but we will also answer some other questions.

What happened in Genesis 1:2?
Why did God not say that Day 2 was good?
When exactly did Adam and Eve sin?
It is highly unlikely that Satan came to Eve as a literal serpent, so in what form did Satan approach Eve?

This understanding and these answers will help us to have a deeper and broader understanding of why God has done what He has done; why He is doing what He is doing; and why He will do what He will do in the future. In the end we know that God has a plan and we can trust Him to work it out and to do all that He has said He will do.

This life is about deciding where we will spend eternity. The Lord Jesus Christ has done everything to save us. To be saved we must believe: "how that CHRIST DIED FOR OUR SINS according to the scriptures; And that he was BURIED, and that he ROSE AGAIN the third day according to the scriptures" (1 Corinthians 15:3, 4).

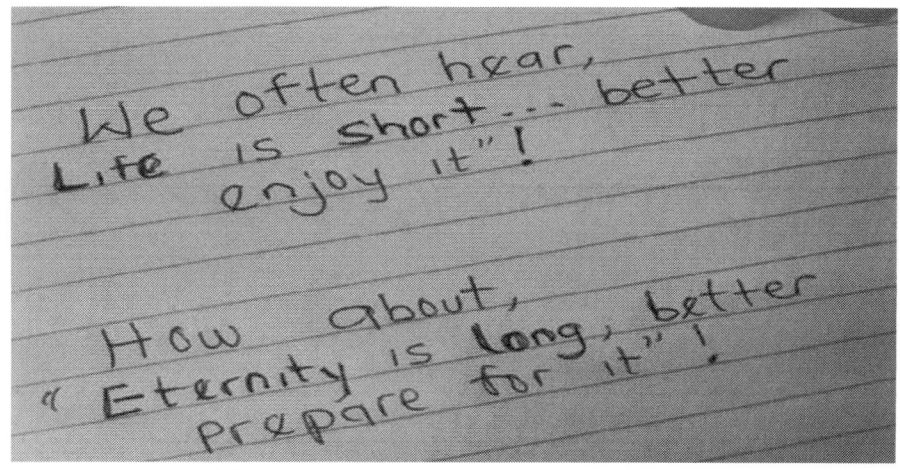

**We are saved by grace through faith, and not by works. Salvation is a gift that needs to be believed in order to be received.**

**"For by grace are ye saved through faith; and that not of yourselves: it is the gift of God: Not of works, lest any man should boast" (Ephesians 2:8, 9).**

<u>**When we believe then we are in Christ, and Christ is in us.**</u> **Christ is perfect, we are in Him who is perfect, and He who is perfect is in us. We have His life in us. The Father now sees His Son's righteousness over us and in us. We are in His Son who lived right. This is how God the Father can then say we are declared right (JUSTIFIED).**

**If we believe, we can expect God to keep His promise to give us eternal life. "In hope of eternal life, which God, that cannot lie, promised before the world began" (Titus 1:2).**

**The apostle John also talked about the promise God made to mankind in prophecy. "And this is the promise that he hath promised us, even eternal life" (1 John 2:25).**

**After we believe and have His Spirit in us we can understand more of what God says in the Bible (1 Corinthians 2:9-16).**

**Faith comes by hearing God's word. "So then faith cometh by hearing, and hearing by the word of God" (Romans 10:17).**

# Eternity

Before God created, before He made anything, He was in eternity. God lives in eternity. "For thus saith the high and lofty One that <u>inhabiteth eternity</u>, whose name is Holy" (Isaiah 57:15).

Eternity is outside creation; it is not within creation. Eternity is not heaven because heaven was created. Eternity existed before God created anything.

Eternity is different from creation. It is called "everlasting." It has no beginning and no end. God's creation is within eternity.

"Before the mountains were brought forth, or ever thou hadst formed the earth and the world, even from everlasting to everlasting, thou art God" (Psalm 90:2).

When Moses asked God what His name was, God said: "I AM THAT I AM" (Exodus 3:14). God is ever present. He is eternal. He said, "I AM." God exists. He does not change. God is outside of time.

There is only one God and there is not any other. God said, "before me there was no God formed, neither shall there be after me" (Isaiah 43:10b).

"Is there a God besides me? Yea, there is no God; I know not any" (Isaiah 44:8).

God said, "for I am God, and there is none else; I am God, and there is none like me" (Isaiah 46:9b).

Time only exists within the creation He made. God is outside time, place, and what He has made. God can see the end from the beginning. "Declaring the end from the beginning" (Isaiah 46:10).

God created a place in eternity for His creation. He created north, south, east, and west (Psalm 89:12; 103:12). <u>God created things in this order: God created (1) heaven, then He created the (2) angels and other angelic creatures, then He created the (3) earth.</u>

"In the beginning God created the heaven and the earth" (Genesis 1:1). (Please note that many modern Bibles put an "s" after heaven making it more than one heaven, which is false. If you have such a Bible throw it away. God's perfectly preserved words are found in the King James Bible). God created a single heaven. It was God's purpose to be one with His creation, to have no barriers between Himself and His creation.

God created heaven and earth by wisdom. "The LORD by wisdom hath founded the earth; by understanding hath he established the heavens" (Proverbs 3:19).

## 1. Heaven

God made a space in eternity and created directions north, south, east, and west. God carved out a place in eternity. God spread out heaven like a curtain, like a tent for Him to live in. "It is he . . . that stretcheth out the heavens as a curtain, and spreadeth them out as a tent to dwell in" (Isaiah 40:22).

This tent has height, width, and length; three dimensions. The tent is made of frozen ice to keep it separate from eternity and cool. It has a bottom (foundation), sides (pillars), and roof (beams). David sang about "the foundations of heaven" (2 Samuel 22:8).

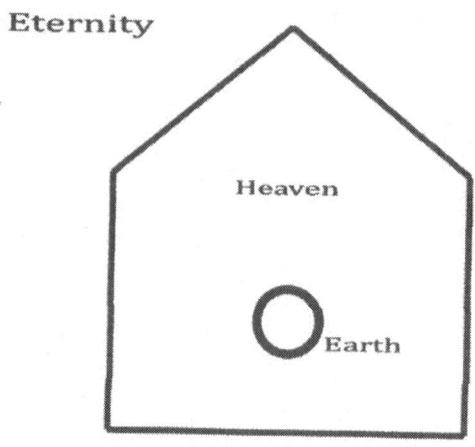

The Earth is Created
and Hung

**God has encapsulated the entire heaven in a frozen shell.** "The waters are hid as with a stone, and the face of the deep is frozen" (Job 38:30). It was God's breath that froze the waters. "By the breath of God frost is given: and the breadth of the waters is straitened" (Job 37:10).

## 2. Angels

**Next God created: The angels (morning stars, sons of God, host of heaven, watchers in Dan. 4:17) and other heavenly creatures.**

**Angels have no wings; Cherubs have four wings; and Seraphim have six wings. God created many different heavenly creatures.**

**The angels must have been created before the earth since the sons of God shouted for joy when God laid the foundations and cornerstone of the earth. God asked Job, "Where wast thou when I laid the foundations of the earth? declare, if thou hast understanding. Who hath laid the measures thereof, if thou knowest? or who hath stretched the line upon it? Whereupon are the foundations thereof fastened? or who laid the corner stone thereof; When the morning stars sang together, and all the sons of God shouted for joy?" (Job 38:4-7).**

# 3. Earth

**God created the earth for Him to live in.**

"For thus saith the LORD that created the heavens; God himself that formed the <u>earth</u> and made it; he hath established it, he created it not in vain, <u>he formed it to be inhabited</u>: I am the LORD; and there is none else" (Isaiah 45:18 compare with Isaiah 40:22).

<u>God created the earth and hung it on nothing.</u> "He stretcheth out the north over the empty place, and hangeth the earth upon nothing" (Job 26:7).

## Trouble in Heaven

"And the <u>earth was without form, and void; and darkness was upon the face of the deep. And the Spirit of God moved on the face of the waters</u>" (Genesis 1:2).

<u>Why was the earth without form and void?</u> What had happened?

This is not how God had created the earth in the beginning. When the angels saw the earth it was light and they shouted with joy.

<u>God had already made earth, water, darkness, space, and the elements before Genesis 1:2.</u> We find the heaven and earth beneath the third heaven filled with water and darkness. <u>But what was wrong? Why was there darkness? God always makes things perfect the first time and He is light.</u>

God, who is light, had left His tent (heaven), made darkness, and drowned the earth. Yikes!!! But why?

God had a plan to deal with Satan and his rebellion and restore what was lost.

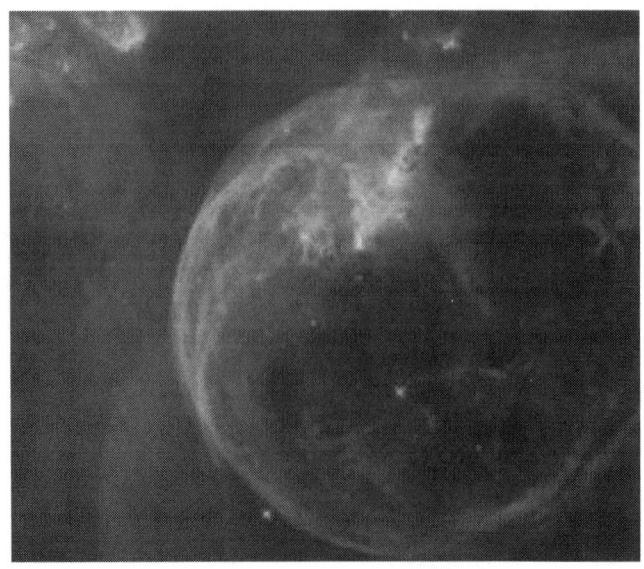

"**And the earth was without form, and void; and darkness was upon the face of the deep. And the Spirit of God moved upon the face of the waters**" (Genesis 1:2).

After God created heaven and earth something very wrong had happened. We can use verses in the rest of the Bible to help us to know what happened. (I have learned so much from the *Scofield Study Bible* and also from the best book I have ever read on the subject, *Creation "In the Beginning"* by Gary Paul Miller. I stand on these men's shoulders.

I have condensed Mr. Miller's 200-page book in a few pages and added some other information. By God's grace the last puzzle piece and some other things have been made clear to me. I want to share the truth I have learned with you so you can have the joy of knowing what God has done, is doing, and will do.)

"God is light, and in him is no darkness at all" (1 John 1:5). God had left the second heaven (withdrew Himself), took His light with Him, and walled off the third heaven with a sea of glass (ice). He put a dark cloud (Job 22:12-14) under that sea so no one could see or go into the third heaven without being invited (Revelation 4:6, 15:2). This made a mirror on God's side. "Hast thou with him spread out the sky, which is strong, and as a molten looking glass?" (Job 37:18).

**The third heaven has a door (Revelation 4:1). Only Paul called it the "third heaven" (2 Corinthians 12:2). Moses and Solomon and others called it "heaven of heavens" (Deuteronomy 10:14; 1 Kings 8:27).**

**Peter said that God destroyed the old earth with water, then remade it, and will destroy the current earth with fire: "all things continue as they were from the beginning of the creation. For this they willingly are ignorant of, that by the word of God the heavens were of old, and the earth standing out of the water and in the water: Whereby the world that then was, being overflowed with water, perished: But the heavens and the earth, which are now, by the same word are kept in store, reserved unto fire against the day of judgment and perdition of ungodly men" (2 Peter 3:4-7).**

"standing out of the water and in the water"

**This flood included "the heavens of old" because the earth was in it. How do we know Peter is not talking about Noah's flood? Noah's flood only affected the whole face of the earth. The earth was never "standing out of the water and in the water" during Noah's flood.**

**How did God overflow the old heavens and the old earth so they perished?** After withdrawing Himself, God let some of the walls of ice around heaven melt and flood the container. The dirt on the earth made the water dark. The heaven was dark without God's light. When the earth was <u>void of inhabitants and empty, God's Spirit returned and "moved upon the face of the water."</u>

The earth was void of creatures. Satan and his angels who were on earth were not on it any more.

<u>Satan said his five "I wills" from earth</u>. "How art thou fallen from heaven, O Lucifer, son of the morning! how art thou cut down to the ground, which didst weaken the nations! For thou hast said in thine heart, *<u>I will ascend into heaven</u>, <u>I will exalt my throne above the stars of God</u>: <u>I will sit also upon the mount of the congregation, in the sides of the north</u>: <u>I will ascend above the heights of the clouds</u>; <u>I will be like the most High</u>*. Yet thou shalt be brought down to hell, to the sides of the pit" (Isaiah 14:12-15). <u>Satan's lie to himself was the deification of the creature</u>. That he could be "like the most high God." Only God is God. Creatures are created. Only God is "the most high God, the possessor of heaven and earth" (Genesis 14:22). Only God is from eternity (Isaiah 57:15). He is the Creator. Created creatures cannot be creators.

The earth was waterlogged (formless). Jeremiah 4:22-28 describes the destruction Jeremiah sees after God's judgment. The words "without form, and void" (Jeremiah 4:23) appear here as the prophet predicts the devastating aftermath of the future Babylonian invasion of Judah. (*Void is uninhabited.)

Jesus told us about Satan when He spoke to the evil religious leaders in Israel. "Ye are of your father the devil, and the lusts of your father ye will do. He was a murderer from the beginning, and abode not in the truth, because there is no truth in him. When he speaketh a lie, he speaketh of his own: for he is a liar, and the father of it" (John 8:44). Satan was a murderer from the beginning. He wanted Adam and Eve to die. He lied to them, to himself, and to the angels.

Satan sinned and that Jesus will destroy the Devil's works. "He that committeth sin is of the devil; for the devil sinneth from the beginning. For this purpose the Son of God was manifested, that he might destroy the works of the devil" (1 John 3:8). Jesus became a man so He could win on the cross by being the perfect sacrifice for our sins and destroy the power of Satan. He is our Saviour.

### God's Plan for Heaven and Earth

"In the beginning God created the heaven and the earth."
God made creatures to live in the two places, heaven and earth.

God wanted His creatures to love Him and trust Him because they wanted to not because they had to. God didn't make them robots. God decided to give His creatures free will.

In a very short time, there was trouble in heaven and trouble on earth. But God was not surprised. He had a plan in place just in case of trouble.

## How did Rebellion Begin in Heaven?

The very first creature to sin was Lucifer, the light-bearer, a beautiful cherub that covered God's throne in heaven (Isaiah 14:12).

God had created Lucifer perfect. Lucifer was in charge of making beautiful music to worship God. Lucifer decided that he wanted to be worshipped like God. <u>Lucifer had a plot</u>. He talked one third of the angels into following him by promising to make them rulers in his kingdom. Cherubs, like Lucifer, have wings and angels do not.

God told Lucifer, "Thou wast perfect in thy ways from the day that thou wast created, <u>till iniquity was found in thee</u>" (Ezekiel 28:15). Iniquity is evil. Evil began in the heart of Satan, not in the heart of God. Spiritual darkness comes from Satan. God told him that the selling of his plan to the angels had made Lucifer violent within.

God knows the thoughts and intents of the heart of His creatures (Hebrews 4:12). God said, "By the multitude of thy merchandise they have filled the midst of thee with violence, and thou hast sinned" (Ezekiel 28:16).

Many of the angels that Satan convinced to join him held top positions in heaven. Gabriel said that only Michael was with him in the truth of what God said. "I will shew thee that which is noted in the scripture of truth: and there is none that holdeth with me in these things, but Michael your prince" (Daniel 10:21). Michael is the prince of the angels for Israel: "the great prince which standeth for the children of thy people [Israel]" (Daniel 12:10).

God said He would cast Lucifer out from where God ruled in heaven. "I will cast thee as profane out of the mountain of God: I will destroy thee, O covering cherub" (Ezek. 28:16). Jesus Christ said "I beheld Satan as lightning fall from heaven" (Luke 10:18).

**Satan was lifted up with pride.** God said, "Thine heart was lifted up because of thy beauty, thou **hast corrupted thy wisdom** by reason of thy brightness: I will cast thee to the ground" (Ezekiel 28:17). It can be inferred that Satan probably sinned shortly after being created. **Satan was a novice that corrupted his own thinking because of his pride.** "Not a novice, lest being lifted up with pride he fall into the condemnation of the devil" (1 Timothy 3:6). **God promised that he would destroy Lucifer** (Ezekiel 28:18, 19).

**God changed Lucifer's name to Satan.** The name Satan, means adversary or enemy. He has other names too, like the Devil, the great dragon, or the old serpent (Revelation 12:9).

**To stop any more angels from disobeying Him, God created a big trash can, called the Lake of Fire.** God prepared the place of everlasting fire for the Devil and his bad angels. The "everlasting fire, prepared for the devil and his angels" (Matt. 25:41).

God cast Satan and the bad angels into the **Second heaven and to the ground**. God sealed off His third heaven with a thick layer or sea of ice (Job 38:30). **The Second heaven is unclean in God's sight** (Job 15:15). God let Satan and his angels be there for now because an empty vacuum is not good and invites worse trouble (Matt. 12:44).

The good angels in heaven decided not to be bad. But Satan and the bad angels were now in the second heaven. In fact, they are still in the heavenly places today. **So there was trouble in heaven and soon there would be trouble on earth.**

Satan was mad. He decided to take as many others with him to the big trash can that he could. Satan is against everything that God does. But God is wiser and stronger than Satan. God also uses Satan to do His bidding (Job 1:12). God uses Satan to find out who really believes God. Believe, faith, and trust all mean the same thing. Faith is believing what God says.

God decided that He would live on earth (Isaiah 45:18).
The earth was without shape and empty; darkness was over the water. And the Spirit of God moved over the waters.

The Son of God spoke everything into being (Hebrews 11:3).

<u>In seven days God "created and made" (Genesis 2:3)</u> the beautiful earth and everything that was in it. There is a difference between "created" and "made." To "create" is to make <u>something out of nothing</u>. "Made" is to make <u>something out of things that already exist</u>. God <u>created</u> three things in the beginning. The LORD God <u>created</u> (1) heaven and earth (1:1), (2) animal life (1:20, 21), and (3) mankind (1:26, 27). God <u>made</u> the rest or brought it forth out of His old creation. We read about the <u>seven days</u> in Genesis chapter 1.

The 7 Days
Day 1 God divides light and darkness. The light was Good.
Day 2 God divides water from the waters.
Day 3 God divides the dry land from the seas. Plants grew. Good.
Day 4 God made the sun, moon, and stars. Good.
Day 5 God created birds and sea creatures and great whales. Good.
Day 6 God brought forth animals and created mankind. Very Good.
Day 7 God rested.

<u>Day 1</u> God divides light and darkness: Day and Night. God's light is allowed back into the second heaven. God divides His light (physical and spiritual) from darkness (physical and spiritual). God may have divided the good angels from the bad. God called the light Day with a capital because it is Day to have the light of God. The darkness was Night. God counts a day from evening to evening (sunset to sunset). A day is a complete rotation of the earth on its' axis. God made time from man's perspective. God said the light was "good."

"3 ¶ And God said, Let there be light: and there was light. 4 And God saw the light, <u>that it was good</u>: and God divided the light from the darkness. 5 And God called the light Day, and the darkness he called Night. And the evening and the morning were the first day" (Genesis 1:3-5). (*Notice that the light was good, not the darkness.)

"God is light, and in him is no darkness at all" (1 John 1:5). Jesus said, "I am the light of the world" (John 8:12).

<u>Day 2</u> God divided the waters from the waters to make the firmament; the <u>first heaven</u> (sky)," <u>the second heaven</u> (outer space). God put the water back into the frozen walls around heaven. <u>God does not call it good</u>. Most probably because, Satan and his angels were again free to move around in this space (Job 15:15). We are told in the Bible that they are there now (Revelation 12:7-9).

"6 ¶ And God said, Let there be a firmament in the midst of the waters, and let it divide the waters from the waters. 7 And God made the firmament, and divided the waters which were under the firmament from the waters which were above the firmament: and it was so. 8 And God called the firmament Heaven. And the evening and the morning were the second day" (Genesis 1:6-8).

<u>Day 3</u> God gathered the waters together and <u>dry land</u> appeared. He called the dry ground <u>Earth</u> and the water <u>Seas</u>. It was good. God let the earth <u>bring forth</u> plants and the trees were big in one day with fruit and seed after its' kind. (Apple trees only produce apples.)

"9 ¶ And God said, Let the waters under the heaven be gathered together unto one place, and let the dry land appear: and it was so. 10 And God called the dry land Earth; and the gathering together of the waters called he Seas: and God saw that it was good. 11 And God said, Let the earth bring forth grass, the herb yielding seed, and the fruit tree yielding fruit after his kind, whose seed is in itself, upon the earth: and it was so. 12 And the earth brought forth grass, and herb yielding seed after his kind, and the tree yielding fruit, whose seed was in itself, after his kind: and God saw that it was good. 13 And the evening and the morning were the third day" (Genesis 1:9-13).

**Day 4** God sets lights in the heaven (the sun, moon, and stars) in order to divide the day from the night, and let them be for <u>signs</u>, seasons, days, and years. The stars make up constellations (Job 9:9; Isaiah 13:10). There are 12 signs (chambers) of the zodiac. One year is a complete circle of the earth around the sun. <u>The idea that the earth is flat is false. It was simply that God often speaks about His creation from a point of view from the earth.</u> God called it good. (Furthermore, men from earth have orbited the earth and moon, have landed on the moon, and then returned back to earth again.) <u>Man does not change or alter the climate on earth. God says the lights He made affect the climate.</u>

"14 ¶ And God said, Let there be lights in the firmament of the heaven to divide the day from the night; and let them be for signs, and for seasons, and for days, and years: 15 And let them be for lights in the firmament of the heaven to give light upon the earth: and it was so. 16 And God made two great lights; the greater light to rule the day, and the lesser light to rule the night: he made the stars also. 17 And God set them in the firmament of the heaven to give light upon the earth, 18 And to rule over the day and over the night, and to divide the light from the darkness: and <u>God saw that it was good</u>. 19 And the evening and the morning were the fourth day" (Genesis 1:14-19).

The heavens display God's wisdom. "The heavens declare the glory of God; and the firmament sheweth his handywork" (Psalm 19:1).

**Day 5** God created fully formed mature creatures like great whales, and birds to fly above the earth in the sky. The chicken did come before the egg. God blessed them and told these creatures to have many babies to fill the water and earth. It was good.

"20 And God said, Let the waters bring forth abundantly the moving creature that hath life, and fowl that may fly above the earth in the open firmament of heaven. 21 And God created great whales, and every living creature that moveth, which the waters brought forth abundantly, after their kind, and every winged fowl after his kind: and God saw that it was good. 22 And God blessed them, saying, Be fruitful, and multiply, and fill the waters in the seas, and let fowl multiply in the earth. 23 And the evening and the morning were the fifth day" (Genesis 1:20-23).

Day 6 God let the earth bring forth land animals and it was good. Then God said let us (God is One God in three Persons) make man in our image. Man is able to reason and has creative abilities. God made male and female. God said that they should rule over the things on the earth and make the other creatures obey them. God blessed the man and woman and told them to be fruitful and multiply, refill the earth, and rule everything that moved. God said that every living thing was to eat plants and seeds for food. God said everything that He made (between Day 1 and Day 6) was "very good."

"24 ¶ And God said, Let the earth bring forth the living creature after his kind, cattle, and creeping thing, and beast of the earth after his kind: and it was so. 25 And God made the beast of the earth after his kind, and cattle after their kind, and every thing that creepeth upon the earth after his kind: and God saw that it was good" (Genesis 1:24, 25).

God created male and female in His own image on Day 6. God says, "let us make man in our image" because He is One in three Persons.

"26 ¶ And God said, Let us make man in our image, after our likeness: and let them have dominion over the fish of the sea, and over the fowl of the air, and over the cattle, and over all the earth, and over every creeping thing that creepeth upon the earth. 27 So God created man in his own image, in the image of God created he him; male and female created he them. 28 And God blessed them, and God said unto them, Be fruitful, and multiply, and replenish the earth, and <u>subdue it</u>: and have dominion over the fish of the sea, and over the fowl of the air, and over every living thing that moveth upon the earth" (Genesis 1:26-28). (*Have complete dominion.)

<u>What were Adam and Eve to subdue?</u> They were to subdue their enemy, Satan. But, as we shall see they failed, instead they were taken in by him.

Meat means food. "29 ¶ And God said, Behold, I have given you <u>every herb bearing seed, which is upon the face of all the earth, and every tree, in the which is the fruit of a tree yielding seed; to you it shall be for meat.</u> 30 And to every beast of the earth, and to every fowl of the air, and to every thing that creepeth upon the earth, wherein there is life, I have given every green herb for meat: and it was so. 31 And God saw every thing that he had made, and, behold, it was <u>very good</u>. And the evening and the morning were the sixth day" (Genesis 1:29-31). (Everything God had made was good, not everything without exception.)

<u>Day 7</u> God had finished His work and He <u>rested</u> from redoing heaven and earth on day seven. <u>God blessed the seventh day and set it apart. That day was the Sabbath.</u> God watered the plants with a mist because He had not yet sent rain.

God had planned to move His house down to earth the following Sabbath (on Day 14). He planned to live with man. But God could not move down to earth because now there was trouble on earth.

## How did Rebellion Begin on Earth?

In Genesis chapter two, God now goes into more detail and tells us how He made the man. "And the LORD God formed man of the dust of the ground, and breathed into his <u>nostrils</u> the breath of life; and man became a living soul" (Genesis 2:7). The nostrils are the holes in the nose. God Himself came to earth to make man. We are "fearfully and wonderfully made" (Psalm 139:14).

God planted a garden in Eden and there He put the man that He had made. "And the LORD God planted a garden eastward in Eden; and there he put the man whom he had formed. And out of the ground made the LORD God to grow every tree that is pleasant to the sight, and good for food; the <u>tree of life</u> also in the midst of the garden, and the <u>tree of knowledge of good and evil</u>" (Genesis 2:8, 9). God told Adam to keep the garden of Eden and to take care of it.

God gave Adam one order. "And the LORD God commanded the man, saying, Of every tree of the garden thou mayest freely eat: But of the <u>tree of the knowledge of good and evil</u>, thou shalt not eat of it: for in the day that thou eatest thereof thou shalt <u>**SURELY DIE**</u>" (Genesis 2:16, 17).

"And the LORD God said, It is not good that the man should be alone; I will make him a help meet for him" (Genesis 2:18). God let Adam name the animals. Adam had the mind of God and named the animals just what God would have. Adam noticed that he was different from the animals. Adam was not an animal. None of them could be his help meet. He was a man made in God's image.

God caused a deep sleep to fall upon Adam and He removed one of his ribs, and then closed him up. Then God made a woman from the rib and brought her to Adam. Adam said, "This is now bone of my bones, and flesh of my flesh: she shall be called Woman, because she was taken out of Man" (Genesis 2:24). God married them.

God told Adam that if He ate of the tree of the knowledge of good and evil he would die. Adam told his wife what God said. <u>Satan didn't want to be subdued by Adam, so Satan developed a plot to defeat Adam and retain the earth.</u>

Satan did not come to Adam; he came to Eve. He said, "<u>Yea, hath God said</u>, Ye shall not eat of every tree of the garden?" (Genesis 3:1). Satan questioned God's word. He made Eve doubt what God said. Satan, with one question to Eve, succeeded in tricking her. He fooled Eve into thinking that she and Adam could be as gods.

Satan lied to Eve. "And the serpent said unto the woman, Ye shall <u>**NOT SURELY DIE**</u> [Satan said the opposite of what God said]: For God doth know that in the day ye eat thereof, then your eyes shall be opened, and ye shall be as gods, knowing good and evil" (Genesis 3:4, 5). Satan said that God knows you will be as gods, and able to rule yourselves without God, if you eat the fruit.

Eve did not say exactly what God said, she left a few words out, and she also added some words. The serpent also questioned and changed God's word. God has said several times in the Bible that we should not add or take away from His word. "Ye shall <u>not add</u> unto the <u>word</u> which I command you, neither shall ye <u>diminish</u> *ought* from it . . ." (Deuteronomy 4:2).

"And the woman said unto the serpent, We may eat [she left out "freely"] of the fruit of the trees of the garden: But of the fruit of the tree which *is* in the midst of the garden, God hath said, Ye shall not eat of it, neither shall ye <u>touch</u> it [she added "touch"], lest ye die" (Genesis 3:2, 3).

The shining serpent (acting on behalf of Satan), "that old serpent," (Revelation 12:9) lied. He tricked Eve into thinking that she and Adam could be as gods (just like Satan wanted to be "like" the most High God, possessor of heaven and earth).

<u>That Eve would have a conversation with a literal serpent is highly unlikely</u>. It is more likely that Satan masqueraded as "an angel of light" (2 Corinthians 11:14). He looked handsome like one of the good angels. "Serpent" is the nature of Satan, not his appearance.

He is sneaky and treacherous "like a snake in the grass." Christ called the religious leaders of Israel serpents and vipers because that was the spirit operating in them. "Ye serpents, ye generation of vipers, how can ye escape the damnation of hell?" (Matthew 23:33). "Ye are of your father the devil, and the lusts of your father ye will do. He was a murderer from the beginning, and abode not in the truth, because there is no truth in him. When he speaketh a lie, he speaketh of his own: for he is a liar, and the father of it" (John 8:44).

Satan beguiled Eve; he dazzled her with his enticing words. She was misled and tricked by the wiles of the Devil. Eve fell for Satan's lie in three ways. Eve thought the fruit would be good to eat. She thought the food looked interesting. She wanted to be wise like God.

Eve took some of the fruit.

## Adam and Eve Disobey God

"She took of the fruit thereof, and did eat, and gave also unto her husband with her. He did eat" (Genesis 3:6). Adam and Eve disobeyed God. They wanted to be like gods and judge good and evil apart from God. God's Spirit in them died. The light inside them went out. They could tell that they were naked. Their bodies that were meant to live forever began to die. Adam and Eve lost the earth to Satan. He remained "the god of this world" (2 Corinthians 4:4); but God says, "all the earth is mine" (Exodus 19:5).

Adam and Eve lost God's Spirit in them. They lost their eternal life. They could not get God's Spirit, His light, back in them by themselves. They could not live forever by themselves. They were helpless and hopeless. Only God could help them. Adam and Eve could not save themselves from the trouble they were in. God would have to do it.

Both human good and evil are bad; we need God's good and right Spirit in us. With the light gone, Adam and Eve saw they were naked, so they sewed fig leaves together to make themselves aprons to cover them.

## Adam and Eve Tried to Hide from God

Then God came as usual to walk and talk with Adam and Eve. They heard Him and hid themselves among the trees. "And they heard the voice of the LORD God walking in the garden in the cool of the day: and Adam and his wife hid themselves from the presence of the LORD God amongst the trees of the garden" (Genesis 3:8).

The LORD God called unto Adam, and asked him, "Where art thou?" (Genesis 3:9). Adam said, "I heard thy voice in the garden, and I was afraid, because I was naked; and I hid myself." (Genesis 2:10).

God knew what had happened but He wanted Adam and Eve to admit they had done wrong. God asked them some questions. God's questions helped Adam and Eve to realize the wrong they had done. Instead of having a wonderful walk with God in the beautiful Garden of Eden they were scared, helpless, and hiding.

God said, "Who told thee that thou wast naked? Hast thou eaten of the tree, whereof I commanded thee that thou shouldest not eat?" (Genesis 3:11).

Adam blamed God and Eve saying, "The woman whom thou gavest to be with me, she gave me of the tree, and I did eat." (Genesis 3:12). We often like to blame others for the wrong things we do. But we need to take responsibility for our actions. Adam did admit that he did eat, he did disobey. We must realize that we have wronged God so we see that we need to trust the solution God has to our problem, and not trust ourselves.

And the LORD God said unto the woman, "What is this that thou hast done?"

And the woman said, "The serpent beguiled [tricked] me, and I did eat" (Genesis 3:13). Eve blamed the serpent, but she also admitted that she did eat.

God said the Serpent would have to eat dust. The LORD God said unto the serpent, "Because thou hast done this, <u>thou art cursed above all cattle</u>, and above every beast of the field; upon thy belly shalt thou go, and dust shalt thou eat all the days of thy life" (Genesis 3:14). God didn't ask the serpent why he did what he did; God knew it was Satan behind the serpent doing the evil. A cherub has a cow or calf face. That is why God cursed him more than other cattle (Ezekiel 1:10, 10:14; Revelation 4:7). The serpent has to eat dust and get around on his belly. God may have said that because he would spend eternity as a dust eating worm, like the rest of his followers.

God promised that the Redeemer would come from the "seed of the woman." The Seed would crush Satan's evil head, killing him, so everything could be right again. Speaking to the serpent God continued, "<u>And I will put enmity [war] between thee [the Serpent] and the woman, and between thy seed [the Serpent] and her seed; it shall bruise thy head [the Seed will crush the Serpent's head a blow that kills], and thou shalt bruise his heel [the Serpent will hurt the Seed's heal, from which He can recover]</u>" (Genesis 3:15).

**God said that Eve would have pain when she had a baby and that her husband would rule over her. Because Adam had listened to Eve, and ate of the tree that God said not to eat of, he had to work hard and sweat in order to have food to eat. The ground was cursed. From now on weeds and thistles would grow in it. Everything God had made had to suffer because of what Adam and Eve did. Adam's and Eve's aprons of leaves would not last. God killed some innocent animals and put their skins on Adam and Eve as their clothes. God spilled the blood of the innocent animals because of the wrong Adam and Eve did.**

**Adam and Eve Have to Leave the Garden of Eden**

**Adam and Eve had to leave the Garden of Eden. God didn't want them to eat from another tree, the Tree of Life, and live forever as imperfect. God put some cherubs and a flaming sword that turned every way to guard the way to the Tree of Life (Genesis 3:24).**

**Life without God was horrible and hard. <u>Adam and Eve finally understood that God's rule was for their protection</u>. They had to suffer because they did not stay within the limit God had set. They had followed Satan instead of God. When they went against God's command, they had joined Satan and his darkness. They joined the rebellion. They should have known that only God is God. They could not be God. The Creator created them. They were made to live forever, but now they were dying. They lost His Spirit in them and their eternal lives. They needed help. <u>Was it too late for them</u>?**

**Adam and Eve believed God would keep His promise and send the "seed of the woman" to rescue them. Adam showed his faith when he called his wife Eve, the "mother of all living" (Genesis 3:20). Adam believed that God could give them back the eternal life and God's Spirit in them which they had lost. Adam believed "the Seed" would come through Eve as God had said.**

## Adam and Eve had Cain and Abel

**God is very clear that Adam and Eve did not conceive until after they left the garden. "And Adam knew Eve his wife; and she conceived, and bare Cain, and said, I have gotten a man from the LORD" (Genesis 4:1). Eve showed her faith when she thought Cain may be the Redeemer. Eve said, "I have gotten a man from the LORD" (Genesis 4:1). Sadly, Cain turned out to be against God; he killed his faithful brother, Abel (Genesis 4:8; Hebrews 11:4). Cain was "of that wicked one" (1 John 3:12).**

**What happened? Cain offered his very best vegetables and fruits to God and Abel offered God his best lamb. God was happy with Abel's gift but not with Cain's. Cain was mad. God warned Cain. Cain did not listen to God. Cain killed his brother Abel.**

## Adam and Eve had More Children

Later Adam and Eve had Seth and then they had many more children because Adam lived to be 930 years old. "And the days of Adam after he had begotten Seth were eight hundred years: and <u>he begat sons and daughters</u>" (Genesis 5:4). <u>Because of their faith, Adam and Eve will live again eternally in God's kingdom on earth.</u>

<u>There is no point in trying to date what God has created, because He made everything full grown and mature.</u> We do not know how long "In the beginning" (Genesis 1:1) lasted. <u>But we can say that it has been nearly 6,000 years since Adam was created.</u>

### Exactly When did Adam and Eve Sin?

When was the Fall of Man? Adam and Eve probably sinned not long after they were made since they had not had any children. I heard Pastor Richard Jordan pinpoint the Fall.

In the chart below the top row is God's days of creation. (He began with "Let there be light".) The bottom row is Adam and Eve's days.

| 1 | 2 | 3 | 4 | 5 | 6 | 7 | 8 | 9 | 10 | 11 | 12 | 13 | 14 |
|---|---|---|---|---|---|---|---|---|----|----|----|----|----|
|   |   |   |   |   | 1 | 2 | 3 | 4 | 5  | 6  | 7  | 8  |    |

Notice that they caused the fall of mankind on Friday the 13th. Day 7 and 14 are Saturdays. The Day before God planned to set up His tabernacle on the earth on the second Sabbath after the first (Luke 6:1). Satan had probably been in a panic to cause man to fall before they had children who could live forever.

How do we know this is true? A woman's cycle is 28 days. She can become pregnant only on one day, the 14th day (14 days after the first day of her period). This is the day that her seed (egg) is available. A man's seed lives from 3 to 7 days. Adam and Eve had probably been together since God married them on Day 6, but her seed had not been available yet (and would not be available for another 6 days).

God tells us that after they left the Garden, Adam knew his wife again and this time his seed joined with hers. She had a baby inside her. "And Adam knew Eve his wife; and she conceived, and bare Cain, and said, I have gotten a man from the LORD" (Genesis 4:1).

In fact, their <u>sin nature spread to all mankind</u>. All humans are born as sinners. "Wherefore, as <u>by one man sin entered into the world, and death by sin; and so death passed upon all men, for that all have sinned</u>" (Romans 5:12). We inherited the sin nature from Adam. <u>A little child knows how to sin from birth</u>. We all need a Redeemer, the Saviour. (Note: There was no death before Adam. Angels never die. God brought forth (or resurrected) the animals again on Day 6.)

Adam and Eve finally trusted what God said. God was their only hope of being able to live with God forever again. <u>God had a plan not only to save them and anyone who believes what He said, but to get the earth back.</u>

Through Paul we learn that Jesus Christ is the Seed: "thy seed which is Christ" (Galatians 3:16). But God wrote the Bible a little at a time, so no one knew that for a long time.

Although Adam and Eve failed to subdue the earth, the Last Adam has succeeded (1 Corinthians 15:45). Paul told us when <u>the Lord Jesus Christ will finally subdue all things</u>. In "the end" he will have put "all enemies under his feet" (1 Corinthians 15:24-28).

Jesus Christ will use the nation of Israel (His Bride) that He will remake from the believing remnant to help Him subdue the earth.

Jesus Christ will use the body of Christ to help Him subdue the heavenly places.

## What is the Last Piece to this Puzzle?

**I believe that in the end, God will hold all the believers in heaven and earth in the third heaven while the rest of heaven and earth will be burnt up. Perhaps this will be by the friction of eternity; God may remove most of the ice walls. Then God will make a new heaven and new earth. He will transport the kingdom on earth believers in the New Jerusalem to the new earth. God will remove the sea of glass and there will be one heaven again with God living with His people. Darkness will be gone, because God is light.**

"Looking for and hasting unto the coming of the day of God, wherein the heavens being on fire shall be dissolved, and the elements shall melt with fervent heat? Nevertheless we, according to his promise, look for new heavens and a new earth, wherein dwelleth righteousness" (2 Peter 3:12, 13).

God removed the sea of ice and made one heaven again. "And I saw a new heaven and a new earth: for the first heaven and the first earth were passed away; and there was no more sea. And I John saw the holy city, new Jerusalem, coming down from God out of heaven, prepared as a bride adorned for her husband" (Revelation 21:1, 2).

All the believers in heaven and earth will have God's Spirit, His life, His light in them and glorified bodies that will live forever (1 John 3:2, 4:13; Romans 8:9; Philippians 3:21). God will rule over the earth through His nation Israel, and over heaven through the body of Christ.

All the Bible is for our learning, but all of the Bible is not written directly "to" or "about us." Most of the Bible is written to and about the nation of Israel. Most of the Bible is about the King and His literal, physical Kingdom on the Earth. The part of the Bible that is directly to and about the body of Christ are Paul's thirteen letters. The letters that all begin with "Paul" (Romans to Philemon).

**Since the present heaven and earth will be burned up, the goal of every person is to make sure they will be in the new heaven and the new earth.**

**How do we get in there? By faith in what God tells us in the Bible to believe (Romans 10:17). Trust God now (1 Cor. 15:3, 4). We do not know how long it will be till the opportunity to live in heaven will last. It ends with the Rapture (when believers go to heaven). It will be almost impossible to believe the truth after the Rapture.**

**God's ultimate plan is "That in the dispensation of the fulness of times he might gather together in one all things in Christ, both which are in heaven, and which are on earth; even in him" (Ephesians 1:10).**

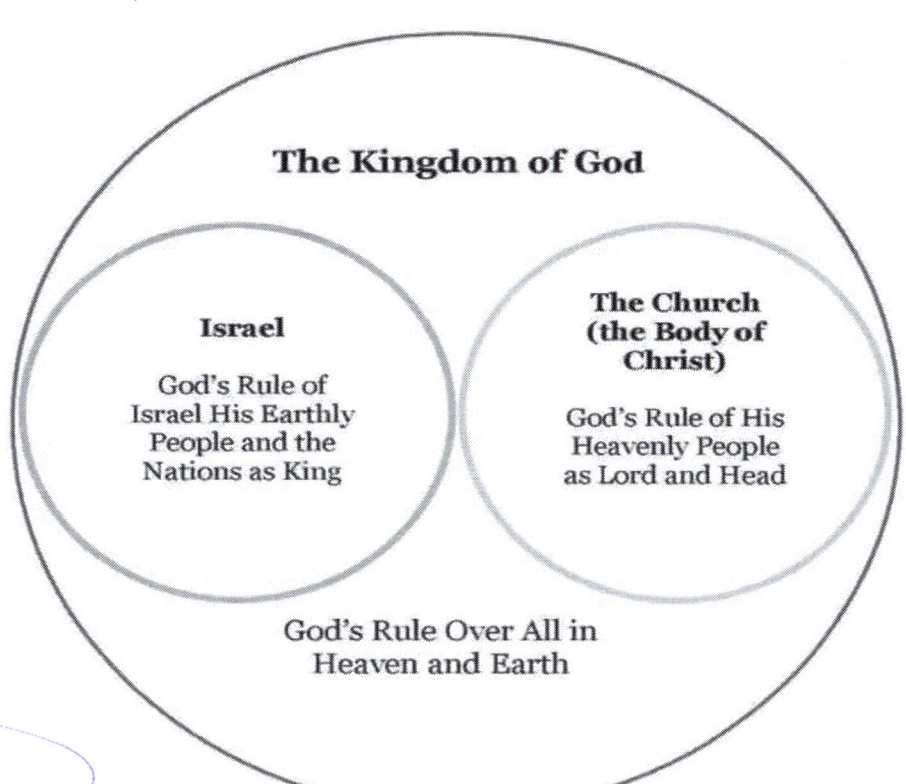

**By one cross, Jesus saved both heaven and earth believers. The believers in heaven and earth will glorify and exalt the Lord Jesus Christ forever. All believers in heaven and on earth will have a part in God's plan to glorify His Son forever (Ephesians 1:11-12).**

**The glory of God is not found except for in the face of Jesus Christ.** "For God, who commanded the light to shine out of darkness, hath shined in our hearts, to give the light of the knowledge of the glory of God in the face of Jesus Christ" (2 Corinthians 4:6). Believers are to reflect His glory to others. We can only do so because we have His Spirit, His life in us (2 Corinthians 4:7, 10, 11).

> And God said, Let there be light: and there was light. And God saw the light, that it was good. . . . —Genesis 1:3-4

### It is all about the Lord Jesus Christ

"I am crucified with Christ: nevertheless I live; yet not I, but Christ liveth in me: and the life which I now live in the flesh I live by the faith of the Son of God, who loved me, and gave himself for me."
GALATIANS 2:20 KJV

# In the first verse
## of the KJV Bible
# God tells us how
# to rightly divide it.

*Genesis 1:1 KJV:*

## "In the beginning God created
## the heaven and the earth."

**God has a HEAVENLY ministry and he has an EARTHLY ministry.**
God has spoken of his earthly ministry since the world began. But, his heavenly ministry was kept secret since the world began, until Christ committed it to PAUL.

## About the Author

**Marianne Manley was saved in 1990. She has more than twenty-five years of experience teaching the Bible. Eighteen of those years were with the AWANA clubs where she earned her Citation Award for Bible memorization.**

**A retired Registered Nurse and Midwife, she has devoted the rest of her life "to make all men see what is the fellowship of the mystery" (Ephesians 3:9).**

**She teaches a Bible study in her home which is available on Facebook and YouTube. The Manley's have three children and live in San Diego.**

**To quickly learn more and to fill in any holes in your foundational understanding of the Mystery read *God's Secret A Primer with Pictures for How to Rightly Divide the Word of Truth.***

**Other Books by Marianne Manley**
Available on Amazon.com in paperback and on Kindle.

*God's Secret A Primer with Pictures for How to Rightly Divide the Word of Truth* (also available in Spanish *El Secreto de Dios*).

*Just as God Said* A children's version of God's Secret with pictures.

*Romans: A Concise Commentary*

*First Corinthians: A Commentary*

*Second Corinthians: A Commentary*

*Galatians: A Commentary*

*Ephesians A Commentary*

*Treasure Hunt Volume I* (Commentary only Romans to Galatians)

*Treasure Hunt Volume II* (Paul's Prison Epistles)

*Could God Have a 7,000 Year Plan for Mankind?*

*AD 34 The Year Jesus Died for All* (same content as Could God, in 9x6 size)

**As a retired Nurse Midwife, Marianne Manley has also written:**

*Birth Stories and Midwife Notes: In God We Trust*

*Born at Home, Praise the Lord!*

*Handbook for Christian Natural Childbirth*

*Christian Childbirth*

The author may be contacted by e-mail at mariannemanley@sbcglobal.net

**Follow her on Facebook at facebook.com/marianne.manley.7 and God's Secret Facebook Page at facebook.com/GodsSecretAPrimerwithPictures. Find her on Youtube (Just type in her name and find her teaching the Bible.)**

**Find her on YouTube (Just type in her name and find her teaching the Bible.) YouTube channel Aaron G. has all of her teachings on Romans to Ephesians will soon have all her teachings a-chapter-at-a-time through Paul's letters (Romans to Philemon). Please visit her website: www.mariannemanley.com**

Made in the USA
Monee, IL
07 December 2019